Old Culross, Valleyfield, Newmills and Torryburn
Guthrie Hutton

Children (and some adults) posing for a camera is nothing new, as this picture of Low Torrie, looking west about 1905, shows.

This picture of the Brae, Newmills, was used as a postcard in 1904, although the photograph may be from an earlier date.

© Guthrie Hutton, 2014
First published in the United Kingdom, 2014,
by Stenlake Publishing Ltd.
54-58 Mill Square,
Catrine, KA5 6RD
01290 551122
www.stenlake.co.uk
ISBN 9781840336726

The publishers regret that they cannot supply
copies of any pictures featured in this book.

Acknowledgements

At various times in my life I have been involved in the activities of the National Trust for Scotland, recreated historical scenes for film making and carried out research into the mining industry, all of which has stood me in good stead while compiling this little book. In digging out the stories I had to call on the help of Fife Cultural Trust, in particular the local history section of Dunfermline Library and Andrew Dowsey at Fife Archives, Markinch. I was fortunate in being able to consult the resources at Cupar Heritage Centre and must also thank my daughter Rowena, whose university studies of pre-industrial historical periods, came to the aid of her old dad. Web sites as ever proved to be useful, if at times frustrating, tools.

Further Reading

The books listed below were used by the author during his research. None are available from Stenlake Publishing; please contact your local bookshop or reference library.

Apted M. R., *The Painted Ceilings of Scotland*, 1966.
Beale, James M., *A History of the Burgh and Parochial Schools of Fife*, 1983.
Dunfermline Co-operative Society, *The Story of the Century 1861-1961*, 1961.
Gifford, John, *The Buildings of Scotland: Fife, 1988*, reprinted 2003.
King, Jessie M., *Dwellings of an Old World Town*, 1909.
Macdonald, Stuart, *The Witches of Fife*, 2002.
MacGibbon, David and Ross, Thomas, *The Castellated and Domestic
    Architecture of Scotland*, Facsimile Edition 1971.
Millar, A. H., *Fife, Pictorial and Historical*, 1895.
Pride, Glen L., *The Kingdom of Fife, An Illustrated Architectural Guide*, 1990.
Silver, Owen, *The Roads of Fife*, 1987.
Thomas, John and Turnock, David, *The North of Scotland*, Vol. 15 of *A
    Regional History of the Railways of Great Britain*, 2nd Edition, 1993.

Introduction

The villages strung along the north shore of the Forth in the past were similar in many ways. People worked at mining coal, making salt and weaving, religion played a big part in their lives, while up on the higher ground the occupants of the big houses created work, levied rents and enjoyed the best views. Then it all changed. Culross, at one time a bustling place of commerce, suffered a perfect storm – literally when the weather destroyed its major industry, a sub-sea coal mine, and metaphorically when the village was left trailing in the industrial wake of developments elsewhere. With its economy in terminal decline through the 18th century, the village sank into a kind of limbo, a shadow of its former self, existing, but not progressing in any way. It became a relic of a time gone by, but by the end of the 19th century people had begun to realise that this was a high value status if only something could be done to preserve it before it was too late. Seizing the opportunity in the 1930s, the National Trust for Scotland moved in to stop the decay and start the process of making Culross into one of the gems in the crown of the nation's heritage.

Valleyfield House and in particular its gardens could have been a heritage jewel, but it was swept away to allow for the development of a big new colliery and its associated village early in the 20th century. The pit was sunk to win coal from some of Fife's most valuable seams, but with its massive headframes and associated buildings it imposed a new landmark on a hitherto little developed coastline. Having altered the landscape, the pit also changed the seascape with waste spreading out from the shore toward the scene of an earlier mining and salt-making enterprise, Preston Island. On the high ground above the pit, the new village of High Valleyfield provided housing for many of the miners and their families, but others found places to live in the neighbouring villages of Newmills and Low Torrie which also developed rapidly to provide the shops and services needed by the vastly increased population.

A new railway was built along the shore, but as it swung inland it formed a physical division between the other villages and Torryburn, which managed to retain much of its character while all to the west was changing. A parish centre, with strongly held religious views and a noted reputation for harrying witches, the village has in more modern times faced pressure coming from the east as better roads, faster cars and proximity to the larger conurbations of Dunfermline and Edinburgh have brought new housing and more people. So under the influences of time, industry, conservation and commuters huge changes have been wrought on a coastal community that was once more unified both in appearance and in the way people lived.

Tanhouse Brae took its name from the local tannery, one of the early crafts practised in Culross. Along with Kirk Street, the steeply sloping thoroughfare forms the link between the low-lying village and the Abbey on the high ground. A more modern picture, taken from the same vantage point, would include the Grangemouth oil refinery in the background, an indication that the Forth estuary has become an industrial powerhouse, as it was when Culross was in its pomp.

Blair Castle, an early 19th century mansion situated to the west of Culross, became a Fife Coal Company property during the First World War when the company bought the estate to obtain the mineral rights. Then, in 1927, the company gifted the house and 28 acres of ground to the Fife, Kinross and Clackmannan Miners' Welfare Committee as a convalescent home. The company also provided £10,000 to help with the costs of refurbishing and furnishing what became known as the Charles Carlow Miners' Convalescent Home, named after the company's former managing director. Initially the home could accommodate 40 guests, but in the 1950s the extensions seen in this picture were completed, increasing the capacity to 70. As the mining industry contracted and convalescent homes in other parts of Scotland closed, Blair Castle became the only establishment offering such facilities to men and women associated with the industry.

Dunimarle Castle, to the east of Blair Castle, occupies a site formerly supposed to be that of Macduff's castle. It is not known if the legendary Thane of Fife did have a stronghold here, but the estate was, for centuries, known as Castlehill and owned by a family named Blaw. About 1830 the estate was sold and then shortly afterwards sold again to Miss Magdalene Erskine, who on marrying Admiral Shairp became Mrs Shairp-Erskine. In the 1840s, while the property was in her ownership, the original 19th century house, on the left, was somewhat overwhelmed by extensions designed by the architects R. & R. Dickson. They added the circular stair tower, adjacent round tower and three-storey wing, all adorned with crenelated parapets, balconies and other Victorian fripperies. With splendid views looking south over the Forth Estuary, few country mansions could have occupied a finer position.

The tower and tops of Dunimarle Castle can be seen screened by trees in the background. In its day, the castle was noted for the splendour of its grounds and especially the gardens, which featured an orangery. Between the foreground houses and the castle is St Serf's Episcopal Chapel, erected in 1876. The church had a chime of three bells housed in the bellcote that can be seen protruding above the roof. When Mrs Shairp-Erskine died she left the great house as the residence of the chapel ministers, also to be opened ocasionally as a museum for her collection of fine art. Over time the house fell into disrepair, the art collection was moved to a new location at Duff House near Banff and in 1970 the chapel was deconsecrated. Restoration of the property began when, in a new century, it was acquired by a new owner.

With the war memorial in the right foreground, Balgownie House is seen here tucked behind its boundary wall. Dating mainly from around 1840, but thought also to incorporate some earlier structural elements, it sits close to where an earlier hospital building stood between 1639 and 1765. The hospital was founded by Sir George Bruce of Carnock (son of the first Sir George) to care for the sick women of the parish. One of the more remarkable features associated with Balgownie House is a stone-built barrel vaulted boathouse situated close to the war memorial. During the Second World War, Balgownie House was used as a hostel to accommodate Land Army girls. After the war it was taken over as a private school. Known as Inchkeith School, the institution had been established in Dunfermline in the early 1950s and moved to Culross in 1959. The school closed in 2003 and the building was restored as a house.

Cut off from the sea by the railway, the Balgownie House boathouse is seen on the right of a picture that, had it been taken in more modern times, would have included the huge Longannet Power Station in the background, but this shoreline has a special place in Scotland's industrial history for another reason. By the late 16th century, the country was suffering coal shortages because the only known method of draining mines was by gravity, and new seams, from which water could be run off, were hard to find. In 1575 George Bruce took a lease on the Culross minerals, but instead of reopening old workings he sank pits, one on land and the other on a tidal island, which was built up around the shaft to above high water mark. Known as the Moat Pit, the level workings between the two shafts were drained using a chain and bucket system driven by a horse gin. It revolutionised mining, produced a vast amount of coal and made George Bruce very rich. He was knighted, taking the title of Sir George Bruce of Carnock, but his wondrous pit was swamped by a storm in March 1625 and shortly afterwards this remarkable industrial pioneer died.

In the days of the Moat Pit people liked to see what they were getting when they bought coal. Only large lumps, 'big coal', could be sold for domestic consumption, but the small bits of coal and dross also had a use. Known as 'panwood' it was burned underneath large iron pans to evaporate seawater and thus make salt, an industry that was carried on in a number of pan houses along the shore. Another coal-burning activity, for which Culross was famous, was the making of iron girdles, products, which along with the coal and salt, needed to be shipped out to markets, so the water between the beach and the Airlie Rocks was partially enclosed by a pier to create a harbour. Boats could be drawn up on the beach, the 'Sandhaven', or come alongside the pier. A wooden walkway to a stone extension were added to the pier, but with the coming of the railway in the early 20th century the old harbour and Sandhaven were filled in. By that time the pier had ceased to be used by all but the smallest of craft as this picture from the Edwardian era shows.

The demise of the Moat Pit was the first of a series of knockout blows to hit industrial Culross. The loss of coal production affected salt making, which although it continued, was doomed to an unequal struggle with cheaper, mined salt from elsewhere and tax changes. Culross had enjoyed an ancient monopoly in girdle making, reinforced in 1599 by King James VI, but no metal workers could compete with the huge Carron Ironworks when it started up on the other side of the Forth on Boxing Day 1760. Big linen factories in Dunfermline likewise rendered the making of cloth on a handloom in a cottage uneconomic. With no money coming into the village, buildings just sat there, getting older. One of these was a malt-house known as the Bessie Bar Hall seen here on the left of a picture from around 1905. Widowed early in life, Bessie was a brewer, quite wealthy and an apparently jolly woman who may have been a close relative of Sir George Bruce. The hall was restored in the 1970s and became a tearoom.

The Culross that slipped into stagnation and decay occupied a narrow strip of ground on the shores of the Forth. Part of the village stretched up the hill to the abbey and church, but the main cluster of buildings was beside the estuary as this picture looking across the roofs shows. Much of what attracted 20th century conservationists is here: buildings that lacked uniformity, irregularly shaped windows and doors, the harled walls, corbie-stepped gables and pantiled roofs. The traditional view of pantiles is that they were imported from the Low Countries as ballast in ships, but it is likely that some, at least, were made locally. Over time they came to be regarded as inferior and were replaced in more prosperous places with slates. In depressed Culross, pantiles remained in use, although the patchwork of tiles, slates and bare sarking on the roof in the right foreground was probably unusual. Clearly in an advanced state of decay, it sits atop one of the finest buildings in Culross: The Palace.

The largest and most impressive historic house in Culross, 'The Palace' is actually a merchant's house, the first part of which was built in 1597; the date is carved on the central wall-head dormer of the building on the left of this picture, along with the owner's initials, GB; mining entrepreneur, George Bruce. His growing wealth and influence are reflected in the larger block, seen here half-hidden by trees, and in the picture on the facing page, which is also topped by wall-head dormers, one of which bears the date 1611 and the initials SGB for the now knighted Sir George. The building was in a parlous state by the late 19th century when architectural historians David MacGibbon and Thomas Ross surveyed it for their splendid five-volume work *The Castellated and Domestic Architecture of Scotland*, published in 1887-92. Their description concluded that it was 'melancholy to see such an interesting structure . . . left to its fate when a few pounds might save (it) for many years'. A saviour, the National Trust for Scotland, appeared 40 years later.

The National Trust for Scotland was set up in 1931 and, encouraged by the Ministry of Public Buildings and Works, acquired The Palace in 1932. The infant Trust then handed the management of the structure to the Ministry, in an arrangement that remained in place through successor government agencies, until 1991. This early 20th century picture shows that the 1611 block was in a bad way when it was taken over, and there was one aspect of the building that needed expert attention; the preservation and restoration of painted decoration. Basing their work on European pattern books, itinerant craftsmen travelled the country painting bright, colourful designs on ceilings and walls in castles, churches and great houses. Examples of this work have been found at a number of locations in Scotland, but the interiors at Culross Palace are amongst the finest to survive. They, along with the external fabric of the buildings, have been carefully restored and, with the National Trust for Scotland taking full responsibility for management of the property, the garden rising steeply behind the 1611 block has also been brought back to glorious life.

In 1588 King James VI made Culross a Royal Burgh, a status that gave the town certain advantages. These included the right to engage in foreign trade and levy charges on neighbouring ports that did not enjoy the same rights, the power to raise taxes for both the national exchequer and local needs, and the right to set up a burgh council. The place where the burgh council met and conducted civic affairs was the tolbooth, or Town House, the building standing sentinel in front of the village, in this view looking to the west. The tolbooth was also used as a courtroom and a prison, and amongst the wrongdoers held within its walls were women who had been branded as witches – a 'crime' that the neighbouring parishes of Culross and Torryburn were more than usually keen to pursue. A stone, dated 1626, is thought to be from when the first element of the tolbooth was built, but the main part of the two-storey block, the entrance stairs and the distinctive tower were erected in 1783.

Outside the tolbooth was the tron, a weigh-beam where people could check that they were being given fair measure, in the days when weights and measures could differ from burgh to burgh. As these became standardised throughout the country, the chalder, the unit for measuring dry volume, was the one from Culross, emphasising how important the burgh once was. Occupying a prominent location at the centre of things, the tolbooth was also close to the harbour side, at a time when the water was closer to the town. Later, when the Sandhaven was filled in and the area in front of the tolbooth became an open space, the building's appearance was, if anything, enhanced. It is seen here in a view looking east toward the village. The building was refurbished in the late 1950s, but the burgh council did not enjoy the benefits for long. In 1975, as part of local government reorganisation throughout Scotland, town councils were abolished and, with no further use for their building, the council gave it to the National Trust for Scotland, which has since utilised it as a visitor centre.

Tucked in behind and to the right of the tolbooth in the picture on the previous page, is the shop, seen here sporting the name of John Penny, general merchant and licensed grocer. The street running away from the camera, Back Causeway, is one of a number in Culross to have the word 'causeway' in the name. Popularly pronounced 'causey', these narrow thoroughfares, far from straight and with uneven building lines, help to give the village its distinctive character. They are surfaced with randomly shaped causeway stones – causeys – and because people in the past used to throw rubbish onto the street, a strip of large flat stones, raised above the others, was laid down the centre of the road to give pedestrians a clean surface to walk on. This 'croon o' the causey' could be straddled by carts, but not cars and so the stones have been lowered for the motor age. People have also become less cavalier about rubbish disposal.

Culross

The fore stair in the centre of this picture of Back Causeway is replicated almost exactly as *The Sunlit Steps*, an illustration in *Dwellings of an Old World Town*, a book of drawings by the artist and illustrator Jessie M. King. Published in 1909, it helped to make people more aware of Culross and its value as a place of historic interest, but failed to preserve the actual 'sunlit steps', which have since been removed. Although undated, the photograph was clearly taken before the 1930s when the National Trust for Scotland started to acquire and restore properties in the village. The process accelerated in 1960 when the Trust launched their 'Little Houses Improvement Scheme', which by purchasing, restoring and reselling houses, aimed to preserve much more of the country's architectural heritage than would otherwise have been possible. What was even more remarkable was that the scheme began at a time when swathes of built heritage were disappearing in the name of 'modernisation'. Much of this 'Little House' activity took place in Culross and some of it in Back Causeway.

At the top of Back Causeway is The Study, seen here in a picture from the late 1930s. Easily one of the finest surviving examples of domestic vernacular architecture anywhere in Scotland, it had become something of a symbol for Culross even before the National Trust for Scotland acquired it. In the late 19th century, architectural historians MacGibbon and Ross (see page 13) found the building so interesting they published two drawings of it (Jessie M. King published three!). The main focus of their illustrations was the distinctive stair tower with its corbelled upper storey, turret and swept dormer windows, which they believed pre-dated the adjacent tenement building. The little room at the top of the tower is what has given the building its name and is thought to be where Bishop Leighton of Dunblane, sat, studied and wrote his sermons.

The Study and the tenement structure to the right of the tower have a dilapidated appearance in this late 1930s picture. Stonework is exposed through broken harling, but some restoration work appears to have done, because the windows, which Jessie M. King drew in 1909 with small paned sashes, have been half-glazed, half-shuttered as they would have been in the early 17th century when the building is thought to have been erected. In the foreground is the market (or mercat) cross which typically for such structures rises from a stepped base to a column surmounted by a unicorn, the heraldic symbol for the Scottish crown and the mark of a Royal Burgh. The base is thought to date from before 1600 while the upper part was made in 1902, at a time when homes in the village were in need of urgent repair. Behind the cross is a house that incorporates a date stone from 1577 and is thought to be the oldest in the village.

At the top of the stiff climb up Tanhouse Brae and Kirk Street is a group of highly significant buildings, seen in this picture from the late 1930s. On the left is Parleyhill House, also known as the 'house with the evil eyes' because of two oval-shaped windows in the gable wall. Just to the right of centre is the gable of the original Geddes School House, but dominating the view is the parish church, built on the site of, and incorporating elements of the former Culross Abbey. Founded in the early 13th century as a Cistercian monastery, parts of the building had been abandoned and others modified by about 1500, with the addition of the tower. The abbey remained empty for some years after the Reformation (1560), but was taken over as the parish church in 1633 and modified twice, once in the 1820s and again, more thoroughly, in 1905. On the extreme right of the picture are the gable wall of the manse and the remains of the old abbey's west choir. The trees and buildings in the middle of the picture hide the Bruce family vault.

To the east of the church is Culross Abbey House, seen here in the late 1930s in a picture that was probably taken at the same time as the one on the facing page. Originally built in 1608 for Edward Lord Bruce of Kinloss, it was enlarged in 1670 by his descendant, Robert, Earl of Elgin, who added a second storey, raised the corner pavilions to four storeys and gave them their distinctive roofs. There was also a wing to the northwest, which suggests that the house was initially intended to surround a courtyard. Through marriage and inheritance, the house became the property of the Earls of Dundonald, but was roofless and had fallen into disrepair when it was acquired by Sir Robert Preston of Valleyfield. He carried out major alterations in 1830 and also modified the northwest wing. In the more modest 1950s the main part of the house was lowered by one storey and reduced in width. The corner pavilions were lowered to a single storey but kept their ogee roofs and were linked to the house by service structures.

Running roughly parallel with Back Causeway is Mid Causeway, seen here looking up towards the Market Cross. At the top of the street, on the left, is a two storey building with attic dormers and projecting sign that was, for many years, a small hotel known as the Dundonald Arms. Planning consent to convert the building into housing was granted in 2008. On the other side of the street was a lodging house used in the 17th century by Bishop Leighton of Dunblane during his visits to the village. At the time the parishes of Tullialan and Culross came under the Diocese of Dunblane because they were in a detached part of Perthshire and not in Fife, a situation that prevailed until boundary changes in 1891. As with other parts of the village, many of the buildings in Mid Causeway have been restored under the aegis of the National Trust for Scotland, although at the foot of the street is one of the more remarkable restorations; a house converted into an electricity sub-station by the then South of Scotland Electricity Board.

The eastern end of the village is seen here in a view looking along Low Causeway, toward Valleyfield. The Geddes School on the right, was built in the late 1860s, but had originally been situated in a house adjacent to the Abbey. Founded and endowed by a Patrick Geddes by or before 1824, with a self-imposed remit of paying for the education of poor scholars, it was not the first place of learning in Culross. A school accommodated in part of the Abbey vault and supported by grants and taxes on heritors (property owning ratepayers) existed by at least the mid 17th century and from this a recognisable burgh and parish school developed. There was also a small subscription school, established by a Miss Farquharson who taught a range of subjects to seven boarders and five day-pupils, and earned more than the parochial teacher. The Education Act of 1872 brought such disparate places of learning under school boards, which were charged with educating all children between the ages of five and thirteen. A new Culross Primary School was built on the site of the Geddes School building in 1961.

Culross Station was opened in June 1906, but the line it was on originated in the intense rivalry between Scotland's big two railway companies, the Glasgow based Caledonian Railway and Edinburgh's North British Railway. Occasionally the two companies put their differences aside, bowed to commercial common sense and negotiated joint arrangements. One such situation arose when the Caledonian proposed to build a bridge across the Forth at Alloa. In exchange for being granted running powers over the bridge, which was completed in 1885, the North British gave the 'Caley' access to their Alloa Station. The arrangement certainly suited the North British; they could run through trains between Perth and Glasgow by way of the Devon Valley line, but the company moved swiftly to thwart any expansion by the Caledonian from Alloa into the Fife coalfields.

The North British Railway blocked the Caledonian's eastern expansion plans by promoting a new line of their own between Alloa and Dunfermline, which effectively duplicated their existing route by way of Oakley. The first section of the new line ran east from Alloa through Clackmannan and Kilbagie to Kincardine, and was opened in December 1893. It stuck at Kincardine for over ten years before being continued through Culross and Torryburn, significantly altering the shoreline, cutting across bays and making it difficult for people to get to rocks and beaches. The completed line was opened in 1906 with four passenger trains a day, each way, and an extra one on Saturdays, but traffic never reached sufficient volume to justify the use of both platforms at Culross, as this picture from a later period than the one on the facing page shows. The service stopped in July 1930, but freight services, or to be more precise, coal traffic kept the line open.

Low Valleyfield, to the east of Culross, developed in the late 18th and 19th centuries with views across the Forth, but that was spoiled in the early 20th century by the new railway, which was built across the bay on an embankment that can just be seen on the right hand edge of this picture. The view has since been totally obscured by the built-up landscape of industrial waste. One of Low Valleyfield's better-known residents, and one of the Geddes School's more famous former pupils, was Stewart McPherson. He left Culross in the 1830s at the age of fifteen, but on discovering that the life of a Dunfermline weaver was unexciting, he joined the army in 1839. In September 1857, having gained the rank of colour sergeant in the 78th Highlanders, he was present at the Siege of Lucknow when he put himself in mortal danger to rescue a wounded comrade and thus became the first Fifer to be awarded a Victoria Cross. When his military career was over, he and his wife settled in Low Valleyfield, in a house they named Lucknow Villa.

Rising up behind Low Valleyfield in the picture on the facing page, is the tree-clad Valleyfield Brae. After the initial steep climb from the coastal strip the ground levels out to a gently undulating landscape where the large and imposing Valleyfield House presided over the surrounding estate, the property of the Preston family since the 16th century. One of the more colourful members of the family was Robert, the 6th Baronet, who inherited the property in 1800 following the death of his brother Charles. Known as 'floating Bob' he amassed a fortune by maritime trading, then inheriting his partner's share of the business, and making a good marriage. He spent some of his money improving Valleyfield, principally by engaging the celebrated landscape designer Humphry Repton to create romantic parkland around the house. It was the only time Repton worked on a Scottish commission and although he didn't actually come north, (his sons did the work on the ground) he created something special, which along with the house, has disappeared.

The principal reason for the disappearance of Valleyfield House and grounds was its purchase in 1907 by the Fife Coal Company, to obtain the mineral rights. The company also secured the mineral rights to the Culross Estate, all of which allowed them to develop a large new colliery on the coastal strip. Two oval-shaped shafts were sunk and by September 1910 they had reached a seam known as the Five Feet seam, which was actually seven feet thick! After digging through another one hundred feet of rock the pit sinkers reached the highly prized Dunfermline Splint seam and by February 1911 Valleyfield Colliery was ready to produce coal. The pit is seen here soon after it went into production. During the sinking operation high levels of gas were encountered and the sinkers had to work by the light of flame safety lamps; it was a sign of things to come because within a month of opening three men were killed when a pocket of methane gas exploded.

Known in the mining industry as 'firedamp', methane was a constant problem at Valleyfield and it had disastrous consequences when, on 28th September 1939, an explosion ripped through the pit killing 35 men. It was the greatest loss of life in a single incident in a Fife pit. Shot firing had ignited the gas, but what made this worse were further explosions of airborne coal dust after the initial blast, a common feature of mine explosions. Collieries generally guarded against this danger by liberally scattering stone dust to damp the coal dust down, but at the subsequent inquiry it was found that stone dusting had been inadequate, an extraordinary situation in a pit known to be gassy. As ever, the wreckage was cleared up and the pit went back to work. On 1st January 1947 the coal industry was nationalized and the colliery became the property of the new National Coal Board (NCB). The NCB planned some improvements, although this picture at the base of number one shaft shows it in 1953 before these had been carried out.

Having started to implement improvements to the existing colliery, a somewhat impatient National Coal Board set about an even more ambitious scheme to more than double the pit's output. This caused alarm with the National Trust for Scotland, which feared that opening up new underground areas could threaten their conservation work in Culross, but in the fuel-strapped 1950s, the NCB was king. They began sinking a new number three shaft to a depth of over 2,000 feet in August 1954; the headframe, made of pre-stressed concrete to resist corrosion from sea air, is seen here under construction in April 1955. The scheme was not even finished when the NCB began a new project, a tunnel under the Forth to link Valleyfield with Kinneil Colliery at Bo'ness on the southern shore. The miners met in the middle on 30th April 1964. By linking the pits together and concentrating coal preparation at Kinneil, the two pits gained a lease of life that carried Valleyfield through to eventual closure in 1978.

The coal industry was in a bad way after the Second World War. There had been little pre-war development and during the war many older pits had been worked to exhaustion. To cap it all, the winter of 1947 was very harsh, so the new National Coal Board had to meet excessive demand with diminished capacity. It was a tough time for the industry, and not wanting to repeat it the NCB planned a number of new super-pits, but because these would take some time to develop they also opened a number of small drift mines to help meet shortages and provide employment for men displaced from older pits. Torry Mine, one of these short-term developments, was designed to produce some 400 tons of coal a day, all of which was sent to the nearby Valleyfield Colliery along the haulage road seen here under construction in 1952. Saleable coal, boiler fuel and mine debris from Torry were deposited in bunkers at Valleyfield, for processing or disposal, a practice that lasted until the closure of Torry in 1965.

In common with other coastal collieries, Valleyfield deposited waste on the foreshore, which built up in the shallow water to create the new land projecting from the shore on the left of this picture. By the time Valleyfield closed, the promontory of waste was being added to by ash from Longannet Power Station and the reclaimed area has continued to grow, to include Preston Island, which can be seen as a distant speck on the right of the picture. At the start of the 19th century, Sir Robert Preston of Valleyfield House built saltpans and sunk pits on the island. With its own coal supply and surrounded by salt water the island was an ideal site to produce salt, but fortune did not smile on the venture. An explosion in one of the pits killed some of the miners, flooded the shaft and consequently reduced salt output. Added to that, tax changes in the 1820s favoured mined salt at the expense of the evaporation industry and by 1850, Preston Island's salt works had ceased production, although the buildings remained in situ as an aid to navigation.

It is hard to escape the conclusion that the big developments along the north shore of the Forth didn't happen in isolation. The railway was built in 1906, hard on its heels the Fife Coal Company started to sink Valleyfield Colliery and, from its Five Feet seam, produce an exceptionally fine steam coal. The Admiralty regarded the Five Feet coal as superior even to the best Welsh coal for powering warships, and they had just established a new dockyard along the Forth at Rosyth. Taken together, this massive activity is therefore more likely to have been driven by coordination than coincidence, but on a purely practical level, none of it would have worked without people, and they needed somewhere to live. Part of the Fife Coal Company's response to this need was to erect 22 of these Viewforth Cottages in 1914/15. With two apartments, scullery and toilet, they were hardly palatial, but better than the miners' rows attached to older pits in the west of Scotland, where many of the Valleyfield men came from.

With Valleyfield Colliery initially employing around 700 men, the 22 little houses shown on the previous page were a tiny percentage of what would be needed for them and their families. Some accommodation was available in the nearby villages, but for the Fife Coal Company there was no alternative to building lots of new houses. They had an ideal site on the old estate; 60 acres of more-or-less flat ground on a plateau above the coastal strip. The company was starting from scratch and with 'garden cities' all the rage – one would soon be built along the coast at Rosyth – they set out to create a 'garden village' at High Valleyfield. Instead of cramming in 25 houses to every acre, they planned just seven, some of which would be laid out in crescents flanking a main arterial road, as seen in this picture of Preston Crescent. The houses in the crescents were to be of two or three rooms, the larger ones having bathrooms and all with back gardens. The oval beds in the middle of the road were planted with shrubs.

These pictures of High Valleyfield are from a slightly later period than the one on the facing page. The upper views show Woodhead Street looking to east and west, while the lower picture shows Preston Street as extended from Preston Crescent. The occupants of the village formed a close-knit community and faced many difficulties together, like the disaster of 1939. Support was strong for disputes, and there were a few of them, but at least one young Valleyfield man, Hugh 'Hughie' Kelly, took a well-trodden route out of mining: football. He played for Blackpool FC between 1946 and 1960, alongside the great Stanley Matthews, and also made one appearance as an internationalist when Scotland beat the USA six goals to nil. As the Valleyfield workforce expanded to over 1,000, the village also grew, with many of the old houses, including the little crescents, being superseded by more modern dwellings.

Newmills got its name from mills first established by the monks of Culross. In those days, monasteries or landowners built mills and installed the miller, but to pay for such big investments, and guarantee a supply of grain, peasant farmers were tied to the mill by a system known as thirlage. They had to take their grain to the mill and were not allowed to do their own milling (although that didn't stop them) and also had to help with the upkeep of the mill, dam and lade. With a percentage of milled grain being kept as payment by both landlord and miller, neither the system, nor the miller were popular, a sentiment reflected in a bitter little rhyme: 'ane tae gnaw, ane tae graw and ane to pay the laird withaw'. Initially at Newmills the 'laird' was the Abbot, but after the monastic lands were taken over by private landowners, the mill at Newmills was renewed at least twice and later became a bleach works. Its smoking chimney can be seen to the left of this picture of Newmills Bridge.

The Bluther Burn, from which the mills derived their power, lost its potency when the mining industry began using the water, spelling the end of the bleach woks. The burn formed the boundary between the parishes of Culross and Torry, and because the former was in Perthshire until 1891 and the latter in Fife, it was also the county border. It was not a particularly formidable barrier and was spanned by a stone bridge of probably 17th century origin. Widened at a later date, it was then superseded by the more substantial bridge seen in the picture on the facing page and fell into disuse and disrepair - part of the old bridge span can just be detected through the arch of the new one. This picture also shows Newmills Bridge, but from street level, with three men wandering along the road in the early 20th century, an activity that would become ever more risky as traffic volumes increased. A man on the left appears to be doing some road or driveway repairs.

Newmills

The Fife Coal Company provided employment at Valleyfield Colliery and housing in their new pit village, but the provision of services was left to others. Just across the parish boundary, Newmills was in an ideal position to cash in and new shops, some of which are seen here on the left, sprang up to cater for the influx of new customers. Also on the left is the West Fife Tavern, a public house set up on co-operative lines whereby a disinterested management was there to serve the customers, but not make profits for themselves. Any money that the venture generated was used to support good causes and village improvements. The idea was based on a Swedish model and such pubs became known as Gothenburgs. A number of these 'Goths' were set up in Scotland following the passing of Industrial and Providential Societies Act of 1897, but the largest concentration was in West Fife. The cottages in the middle of the picture and seemingly in the middle of the road were erected, according to the marriage lintels above the two front doors, in 1712.

It is not known when the Wardlaw family took possession of the lands that made up the Torrie estate, but they appear to have been in their possession for a long time, before Colonel William Erskine acquired the estate in 1689. He was the first of three William Erskines to hold the estate, the second of whom was wounded at the Battle of Fontenoy in 1745 and the third, a Lieutenant General, was awarded a knighthood in 1763 and a baronetcy in 1791. A succession of Erskines followed, including Sir John Drummond Erskine who bequeathed a collection of paintings and sculpture from Torrie House to the National Galleries in Edinburgh. Successive Erskine lairds developed Torrie House into the grand mansion seen in this picture and Admiral Sir James Erskine Wemyss is credited with laying out the grounds in the 1820s. About 100 years later, part of the estate was laid out as a golf course for the Dunfermline Golf Club, by James Braid from Elie, one of the finest course designers of his generation.

The flanking wall to the Torrie House gateway is seen on the extreme left of the upper of these pictures showing the Newmills Brae. The scarcely prominent road sign, warning motorists of the steep hill, has since been removed – perhaps the traffic calming effect of parked vehicles has made the Brae is less hazardous. With the Crown Hotel on the right, the lower picture looks west up the Brae. On the left is the distinctive ogee-roofed corner of the Dunfermline Co-operative Society building, which was opened in March 1911 by the President of the Society, George Wright. He urged villagers to support the store, which they did to such an extent on the opening day that it stayed open beyond normal closing time, selling the co-op's usual range of groceries along with clothing, boots and shoes. Two months later, the Society, which was founded in January 1861, celebrated its silver jubilee with a parade through Dunfermline followed by sports, band music and public dancing.

To the east of the Brae, at Low Torrie, the road levels out with, on its south side a tenement block (see back cover), facing the individual houses seen here, to the north. These contrasting buildings reflect changing lifestyles, with the more scattered housing redolent of the weaving industry that occupied many villagers before large-scale mining brought a new population of industrial workers. The picture dates from around 1905 and appears to have been taken from the railway embankment, then under construction. Before the railway reduced its size and amenity, the beach was evidently an attractive place but, at one time, it was the last place a woman would want to be seen, because this was where Torryburn's witches were tortured or buried. Some men were accused, but the usual suspects were widows or spinsters, women in what some people at the time regarded as the unnatural state of being unmarried and because such wrongdoers could not be buried in consecrated ground they were disposed of on the foreshore between the low and high tide lines.

Low Torrie

Having voted in favour of setting up a library under the provisions of the Public Libraries Consolidation (Scotland) Act of 1887, local people were delighted when, about a month before Christmas 1910, Andrew Carnegie announced his intention to give £1,000 to the project. A site to the west of Tinian House was secured and, with designs already prepared by William Ramage of Dunfermline, building work started quickly. There was to be a library, ladies' room and a hall that could accommodate 380 people, and the plans allowed for expansion when funds permitted. On a boisterous day in early November 1911, Dr. Ross, chairman of the Carnegie Dunfermline Trust, opened the new facility and as a memento of the occasion, Mr Ramage presented him with a silver key. Just before Christmas 1911 the Dunfermline Co-operative Society hosted a concert with a comedy act, songs, music and a bioscope entertainment. It was typical of the way the hall quickly became an important part of village life, able to host concerts, dances, fund raising events and the activities of local clubs and societies.

Within months of the hall's opening, work to build a new school began on a nearby site. The existing school, which consisted of two old classrooms, two new rooms and a hall, could accommodate 212 pupils, but with the population of the area growing rapidly as a result of industrial development, the Parish of Torryburn School Board engaged Dunfermline architect John Houston to look at the options of either expanding the old school or building on a new site. He recommended the latter, selecting Tinian Park as the preferred location. The new school was designed to accommodate over 300 pupils in six classrooms, with rooms available for lessons in cookery, laundry work and manual trades. These could also be used as auxiliary classrooms, should the need arise. In April 1913, a large crowd gathered in the central hall to witness Mrs. Miller, wife of the chairman of the School Board, open the new school. After the speeches and presentations the gathering was treated to a programme of recitations, singing and dancing given by the children, under the direction of the headmaster, Mr Beveridge.

Having imposed their railway on the coastal strip between Culross and Low Torrie, the engineers swung it inland on an embankment and, despite bridging the road, formed a physical division between Low Torrie and Torryburn. The line also of course gave access to the wider world with a Torryburn Station built on Tinian Park. It is seen here shortly after its opening in 1906, with Tinian House in the background. As well as regular services, special trains were put on to take local groups on outings to places like Tulliallan, while trippers from elsewhere came to Torryburn for picnics. Some local people were not happy with the level of service offered by the North British Railway and four years after the line's opening petitioned them to put on an early morning train so that Torryburn workers could get to the Dunfermline linen factories. The petitioners also suggested a return service to the seaside for day-trippers, but while the company did not immediately reject the idea, their focus seems to have been more on moving coal than people.

Held on the second Wednesday of July, the annual Torryburn Fair was a typical country fair, with the added incentive of a horse race at the end of the day. Streetwise traders, with strange sounding names, arrived to hawk their wares to unsuspecting country folk. They wheeled barrows of fruits and berries, carried baskets of household goods or potions, pastes and powders to cure toothache, root out corns, remove warts or if all that failed, to polish the furniture. With attractions like the intelligent pig, whistling monkey and the musical horse, excitement was in the air, helped by the intermingled sounds of the hurdy-gurdy, fiddlers, pipers or fife players. Just before the First World War the fair had become a sideshow to an annual sports event. The railway had taken over the traditional fairground at Tinian Park and the merry-go-rounds, stalls and caravans occupied the foreshore as seen here in a photograph taken from the railway embankment. It was used as a postcard in March 1910, so it must date from one of the years between 1906 and 1909.

A Torrie Hotel had been catering for travellers and village drouths before 1897, the date inscribed above the door of this building. Conveniently situated on the main road, the hotel was also ideally placed when the station was built a short walk away. The proprietor, Mr Buist, must have been a determined man to operate licensed premises in a village where attitudes to strong drink were, at best, ambivalent. At the opening of the library and hall, when village institutions were praised, regret was expressed at the existence of public houses. In the 1840s, the Rev. Thomas Doig, who wrote the *New Statistical Account*, praised a Mr Beveridge of Inzievar House for his 'enlightened interference' in attempting to curtail the consumption of the demon drink. Much of this opposition had its roots in strong religious beliefs. The village was at the heart of Torryburn parish, which was formed some time around the early 17th century with the union of the earlier parishes of Torry and Crombie. The boundaries were set in 1890 when two detached portions of Saline and Torryburn parishes were swapped.

The Parish Church is in the background of this view of Main Street, taken from a spot close to the former Torryburn Post Office, which was run between the 1860s and 1950s by one man and then his daughter, who continued to act as postmistress long after retirement age. Another lady who lived to a ripe old age was Alison Cunningham. Born in Torryburn in 1822, she moved to Edinburgh where she became Robert Louis Stevenson's boyhood nurse in 1852. He dedicated his book *A Child's Garden of Verses* to her. She grew up imbued with the strong religious traditions of a village with the church at its heart. Rebuilt in 1800 and reconstructed in 1928, the church could seat a congregation of 502, but in 1843, when the great schism known as the Disruption split the Established Church of Scotland, about eighty per cent of Torryburn's parishioners, a significantly higher proportion than the national average, left the old church, along with the Rev. Doig, to form a congregation of the newly created Free Church. They met for worship in a shed fitted up with a pulpit and seats until a new church could be built.

These pictures show the Parish Church and the manse, a building that dated mainly from the late 1760s, but with a taller mid 19th century extension, to the right. Torryburn Church would have been noted simply as a place of worship, had it not been for its witch-hunting activities. Vigorously pursued in the 17th century, the practice spread into the early 18th century thanks to the activities of the Rev. Alan Logan. Women, accused by him, admitted to being at a meeting of witches beside the churchyard, having a compact with the devil and to seeing his cloven feet, like those of a cow. In 1704 one woman, Lilias Adie, having confessed to consorting with the devil, died in Dunfermline jail and was buried on the foreshore. Another woman, Helen Kay, who disagreed with the Rev. Logan, was publicly rebuked in April 1709 for calling him 'daft', but does not appear to have suffered the same fate as Lilias Adie, so perhaps by that time people were beginning to believe that tormenting people into confessing to witchcraft was indeed daft, and cruel.